Dainty Sweets

Ices, Creams, Jellies, Preserves

by

Archie Corydon Hoff

APPLEWOOD BOOKS
Bedford, Massachusetts

Dainty Sweets

was originally published in

1913

ISBN: 978-1-4290-1043-6

Thank you for purchasing an Applewood book.
Applewood reprints America's lively classics—
books from the past that are still of interest
to the modern reader.
For a free copy of
a catalog of our
bestselling
books,
write
to us at:
Applewood Books
Box 365
Bedford, MA 01730
or visit us on the web at:
For cookbooks: foodsville.com
For our complete catalog: awb.com

Prepared for publishing by HP

Dainty Sweets

ICES,
CREAMS, JELLIES, PRESERVES

By the

WORLD FAMOUS CHEFS
United States
Canada
Europe

The Dainty Sweet Book

From the

INTERNATIONAL COOKING LIBRARY

Compiled and Edited by
A. C. HOFF

Los Angeles, Cal.
International Publishing Co.
1913

AGRICULTURE

CONTRIBUTORS

Emile Bailly, Chef..........Hotel St. Regis..........New York City
Jean S. Berdou, Chef.......Hotel Astor..........New York City
Jean Millon, Chef..........Ritz-Carlton..............New York City
Henry Berger, Chef.........Frankfurter-Hof.........Frankfurt, Germany
Jules Kohler, Chef..........Hotel Adlon..............Berlin, Germany
G. Milhau, Chef............Tait-Zinkand Cafe.......San Francisco
Adrian Delvaux, Chef.......Hotel Baltimore.........Kansas City
Otto Geutsch, Chef.........Hotel Windsor...........Montreal
Joseph D. Campazzi, Chef....Royal Poinciana.........Palm Beach
E. C. Perault, Chef..........Planters Hotel............St. Louis
John Chiappano, Chef......Auditorium Hotel........Chicago
Geo. R. Meyer, Chef........Rector's Cafe............Chicago
Gerard Embregts, Chef......Chateau Frontenac......Quebec
Louis Pfaff, Chef..........New Willard Hotel....·....Washington
Henry Johannsen, Chef.....Hotel Royal Palm........Miami
Victor Hirtzler, Chef........Hotel St. Francis........San Francisco
Emile Burgermeister, Chef...Hotel Fairmont..........San Francisco
Martin Ginder, Chef........Hotel Green.............Pasadena
Joseph Stoltz, Chef.........Hotel Ponce de Leon.....St. Augustine
Henri Boutroue, Chef.......Hotel Shelbourne........Dublin, Ireland
Thos. Cooney, Chef.........Van Nuys Hotel.........Los Angeles
Jules Dauviller, Chef........Palace Hotel.............San Francisco
Arthur Taylor, Chef........Hotel Raymond..........Pasadena
Ernest Otzenberger, Chef ...Hotel Dennis............Atlantic City
Cesar Obrecht, Chef........Grand Hotel de L'Europe Lucerne, Switzerland
Jules Boucher, Chef.........Arlington Hotel..........Hot Springs
Chas. Grolimund, Chef.....Washington Hotel.......Seattle
Jean Juillard, Chef.........Hotel Adolphus..........Dallas
Chas. Pier Giorgi, Chef.....Hotel Alcazar............St. Augustine
Peter Bona, Chef............Hotel Chamberlain......Fortress Monroe
Louis Lescarboura, Chef.....Ft. Pitt Hotel............Pittsburgh
John Pfaff, Chef............Hotel Cape May.........Cape May
Walter Jurenz, Chef........Hotel Galvez.............Galveston
S. B. Pettengill, Chef.......Hotel Ormond...........Ormond Beach
Geo. E. Schaff, Chef........Hotel Albany............Denver
Ben E. Dupaquier, Chef.....Hotel Arlington..........Santa Barbara
William Leon Benzeni, Chef .Hotel Virginia..........Long Beach
Chas. A. Frey, Chef.........Hotel Alexandria.........Los Angeles
Lucien Fusier, Chef.........Grand Hotel Metropole...Interlaken, Switzerland
G. Cloux, Chef..............U. S. Grant Hotel........San Diego
A. Schloettke, Chef.........Westminster Hotel.. .....Dresden, Germany
Lucien Raymond, Chef......Hotel Congress & Annex..Chicago
Louis Thein, Chef...........Hotel Utah...............Salt Lake City
Jules Edward Bole, Chef....Hotel Jefferson...........St. Louis
John Bicochi, Chef..........Hotel Piedmont..........Atlanta
Edw. R. J. Fischel, Steward ..Hotel Piedmont.........Atlanta,
Leopold Saux, Steward......Hotel Grunewald........New Orleans
Henri D. Fouilloux, Steward..St. Charles Hotel........New Orleans

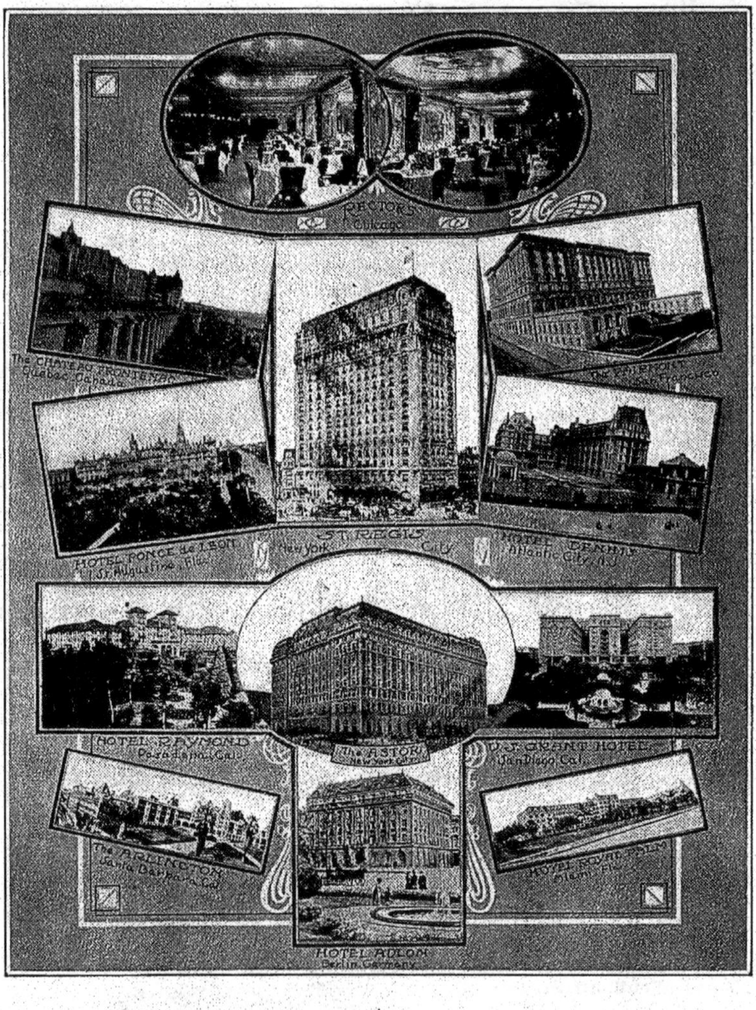

5

THEIR CHEFS-OUR CONTRIBUTORS

PREFACE

In presenting this book on DAINTY SWEETS to the public, we feel that we are presenting the most complete authorative and up-to-date book ever prepared on the subject. The contributors being the finest chefs in the United States, Canada and Europe insure every recipe shown as right. These world famous chefs have given us their special recipes and they have made the explanations so plain and so complete that any one can readily understand them.

The great chefs who have prepared these recipes for us have all made cooking their life work and have been apprenticed under the finest and most practical teachers in the culinary lines in this country and abroad.

A large portion of the copy has been translated from the French. The finest chefs are generally the French or Swiss. They are not literary men; their language is not flowery, but we know that even with the difficulty that exists in expressing in English many of the French terms that the work as a whole will be easily understood and greatly appreciated.

This is the first time in history that such a wonderful collection of recipes has been made obtainable for general use. These men are giving, in these recipes, their "professional secrets." The calibre of the men who have prepared these recipes is as great and represents as much as the great masters in other lines of the world's work. Napoleon Bonaparte was a great general; Shakespeare, a great author; George Washington, a wonderful statesman; and Thomas Edison, a masterful inventor; but we feel that the master chefs represented here are to be considered just as great and doing just as much of the world's work as any of the famous men we have all been taught to revere and respect.

The International Cooking Library, covering in ten volumes, every conceivable part, section or angle of the cooking question makes

THEIR CHEFS—OUR CONTRIBUTORS

it possible for any one who will follow these recipes to be an expert cook. The great masters who have prepared these recipes have spent their lives studying and experimenting and are giving in these recipes their best ideas and suggestions. These are dishes of the millionaires and the most particular epicureans.

We feel that this set of books is presented to the public at just the opportune time. All people are beginning to realize that there is really no more important art than cooking and this should be so; for what should be considered more important than what we eat? The best health insurance is having the right kind of foods, properly prepared. A man is at his best only when he is in robust health and nothing will undermine a person's constitution so quickly as poor food. The best dishes and the sure and absolute recipes for making them are contained in this wonderful set of books. All the copy is from authorities just as positive and just as sure in this line as the noted Blackstone was on legal lines. We picked the best chefs in the world; we would accept copy from no others.

A careful study of the recipes and careful application of the directions for same is all that is necessary to produce the results that have made these men famous.

In the presentation of this book, we wish only that space would allow us to mention and pay courtesy to the many men who have assisted us in the various departments, copy preparation, translation, and editing, also the courtesies rendered by the managers of the world-renowned hotels whose chefs have been our contributors.

INTERNATIONAL PUBLISHING COMPANY.

INDEX

JELLIES, PRESERVES AND SWEETS

PAGE

VICTOR HIRTZLER, Chef de Cuisine, ST. FRANCIS HOTEL, San Francisco, Cal . . . 15

STRAWBERRY PRESERVES
BLACKBERRY JAM
RASPBERRY OR LOGANBERRY
  JAM
CANNED STRAWBERRIES
APPLE JELLY
CURRANT JELLY
CRANBERRY JELLY
CRAB APPLE MARMALADE
  AND JELLY
APRICOT MARMALADE
BRANDIED CHERRIES
BRANDIED PEACHES
PRESERVED CHERRIES
PRESERVED GAGE PLUMS
QUINCE JELLY
PRESERVED PEARS
PINEAPPLE PRESERVES
CITRON PRESERVES
WATERMELON PRESERVES
CANNED PEARS, PEACHES OR
  PLUMS
CANNED PEACHES
CANNED APPLES AND
  QUINCES
CANNED PEARS
TOMATO PRESERVES
APPLE BUTTER
CALIFORNIA MARMALADE
GRAPE JELLY
GOOSEBERRY JAM

SPICED VINEGAR FOR
  PICKLES
SPICED CHERRIES
SPICED SWEET APPLES
SPICED TOMATOES
NASTURTIUMS
PICKLED ARTICHOKES
PICKLED ONIONS
PICKLES
SWEET PICKLED PEACHES
GREEN TOMATO PICKLE
RIPE CUCUMBER SWEET
  PICKLE
SWEET GRAPE JUICE
PRESERVED VIOLETS
CANNED MINCEMEAT
TO CAN PUMPKIN OR SQUASH
TO PRESERVE LIMES
JELLIED CHERRIES
CANDIED LEMON OR ORANGE
  PEEL
FIG JAM
BLACKBERRY CORDIAL FOR
  MEDICINAL PURPOSES
VANILLA BRANDY
ORANGE OR LEMON BRANDY
  FOR FLAVORING
GLACES—FRUITS
BAKED PEARS FOR CANNING
RASPBERRY JUICE
BOILED CIDER

SWEETS

ERNEST OTZENBERGER, Chef de Cuisine, HOTEL DENNIS, Atlantic City, N. J . . 42
  MOUSSE A LA VANDERBILT   VIRGIN STRAWBERRY CREAM

HENRI BERGER, Chef de Cuisine, FRANKFURTER-HOF, Frankfurt, Germany. . . . 53
  PECHES CARUSO

ADRIAN DELVAUX, Chef de Cuisine, BALTIMORE HOTEL, Kansas City, Mo. . 37
  GRAPE FRUIT ICE   COUPE NANNETTE
  ICE CREAM A LA BALTIMORE   GLACE A L'HARANAISE
  PUNCH VICTORIA   PUNCH A L'IMPERIALE
    BALTIMORE SHERBET

HENRI BOUTROUE, Chef de Cuisine, HOTEL SHELBOURNE, Dublin, Ireland. . 40
  BOMBE TOGO

G. MILHAU, Chef de Cuisine, TAIT-ZINKAND CAFE, San Francisco, Cal 36
  TARTELLETTES CALIFORNIA   GLACE PRALINES
  BOMBE NELUSKO   CHAMPAGNE SHERBET
    MOUSSE OF CHOCOLATE

THEIR CHEFS-OUR CONTRIBUTORS

WALTER JURENZ, Chef de Cuisine, HOTEL GALVEZ, Galveston, Tex.......... 43
   FRENCH APPLE TARTE,   STARS AND STRIPES BANNER PUNCH
        OLD FASHIONED COFFEE PARFAIT

CESAR OBRECHT, Chef de Cuisine, GRAND HOTEL DE L'EUROPE, Lucerne,
   Switzerland... 41
        MOUSSE DAME BLANCHE

CHAS. PIER GIORGI, Chef de Cuisine, HOTEL ALCAZAR, St. Augustine, Fla.... 35
   SHERBET A' LA'DUSE   BOMBE TRIUNWIR

LUCIEN FUSIER, Chef de Cuisine, GRAND HOTEL METROPOLE, Interlaken,
   Switzerland... 45
        BOMBE EXCELSIOR

VICTOR HIRTZLER, Chef de Cuisine, ST. FRANCIS HOTEL, San Francisco, Cal .. 31
   MACEDOINE WATER ICE   BURGUNDY PUNCH
   NORMANDY WATER ICE   CARAMEL ICE CREAM
   SORBET A EAU DE VIE DE   BANANA ICE CREAM
    DANTZIG   FRESH RASPBERRY PUNCH
   SORBET PARLERMENTAIN   BISCUIT GLACE ST.
   VICTORIA PUNCH   FRANCIS

LUCIEN RAYMOND, Chef de Cuisine, HOTEL CONGRESS AND ANNEX,
   Chicago, Ill.. 48
   POIRE MARY GARDEN   PEACHES GLACES WILHELMINE
   NEIGE AU CLIQUOT   COUPE CZARINE

JEAN JUILLARD, Chef de Cuisine, HOTEL ADOLPHUS, Dallas, Texas.......... 56
   COUPE CIGARETIERRE   CHOCOLAT CHANTILLY

JOHN BICOCHI, Chef de Cuisine, HOTEL PIEDMONT, Atlanta, Ga...:........ 46
   SHERBET PARFAIT D. AMOUR   BAVAROISE EN BELLEVUE

JULES BOUCHER, Chef de Cuisine, ARLINGTON HOTEL, Hot Springs, Ark.... 57
        BANANA SOUFFLE RUSSE

JULES DAUVILLER, Chef de Cuisine, PALACE HOTEL, San Francisco, Cal... 50
   MERINGUES PANACHEES   MOUSSE AUX FRAISES ROMANOFF
      PUNCH GRANITE A L'ANANAS

JULES KOHLER, Chef de Cuisine, HOTEL ADLON, Berlin, Germany.......... 59
    SURPRISE DES CHARTREUX

GERARD EMBREGTS, Chef de Cuisine, CHATEAU FRONTENAC. Quebec, Can.. 53
      BAVAROIS AUX FRAISES

LEOPOLD SAUX, Chef de Cuisine, HOTEL GRUNEWALD, New Orleans, La...... 54
        ORANGE PUNCH

EMILE BURGERMEISTER, Chef de Cuisine, HOTEL FAIRMONT, San Francisco,
   Cal.. 47
   PINEAPPLE COUPE AU HIRSH   MARQUISE CALIFORNIA
      STRAWBERRY ROMANOFF

LOUIS LESCARBOURA, Chef de Cuisine, FT. PITT HOTEL, Pittsburg, Pa........ 56
   PUNCH DELICES   COUPE FAVORITE

JOHN CHIAPPANO, Chef de Cuisine, AUDITORIUM HOTEL, Chicago, Ill...... 40
            PEACHES A LA TORINESE

BEN E. DUPAQUIER, Chef de Cuisine, HOTEL ARLINGTON, Santa Barbara, Cal., 49
    MARRON ICE CREAM   VANILLA ICE CREAM

GEORGE R. MEYER, Chef de Cuisine, RECTOR'S CAFE, Chicago, Ill.......... 58
     PUNCH AU PARFAIT AMOUR
     SURPRISE PYRAMID, NAPOLITAINE
     FRENCH VANILLA ICE CREAM
     ALPS GLORY

MARTIN GINDER, Chef de Cuisine, HOTEL GREEN, Pasadena, Cal............ 51
    TUTTI FRUITTI PUNCH   ORANGE SHERBET
          PISTACHIO ICE CREAM

OTTO GEUTSCH, Chef de Cuisine, HOTEL WINDSOR, Montreal, Can.......... 55
    SOUFFLE PALMYRE   PECHES POLE DU NORD

JOSEPH P. CAMPAZZI, Chef de Cuisine, ROYAL POINCIANA, Palm Beach, Fla .. 52
      COMPOTE OF PEACHES A LA VAN DYKE

LOUIS THEIN, Formerly Chef de Cuisine, HOTEL UTAH, Salt Lake City, Utah.. 3[8]
    STRAWBERRY ICE CREAM   TUTTI FRUITTI ICE CREAM
          BAKED ALASKA

HENRI D. FOUILLOUX, Chef-Steward, ST. CHARLES HOTEL, New Orleans, La .. 54
        COUPE ST. CHARLES

EMILE BAILLY, Chef de Cuisine, HOTEL ST. REGIS, New York City, N. Y.... 44
    PONCIRE PRINTANIERE   CREAM GLACE BONNE MAMA
          MERINGUES GLACE

EDMOND C. PERAULT, Chef de Cuisine, PLANTERS HOTEL, St. Louis, Mo.. 39
    PUNCH MOS COWITE   SORBET AUX PECHES
        GRANITE AUX ANNANAS

CHARLES A. FREY, Chef de Cuisine, ALEXANDRIA HOTEL, Los Angeles, Cal., 33
     STRAWBERRY MOUSSE
     ICED TEA
     CAFE PARFAIT ALEXANDRIA
     ICE CREAM YOKOHOMA
     CHOCOLATE MOUSSE ANNA HELD
     ICE CREAM AL'IMPERATRICE
     ORANGE ICE COVINA
     BAVAROIS OF APRICOTS

VICTOR HIRTZLER
Chef de Cuisine
ST. FRANCIS HOTEL
SAN FRANCISCO

VICTOR HIRTZLER
CHEF DE CUISINE
HOTEL
ST. FRANCIS
San Francisco, Cal.

Mr. Hirtzler was born in Strasbourg, Alsace, Germany, and learned his profession under Emile Feypell in Strasbourg who is considered one of the finest Chefs in France. Mr. Hirtzler has been in the best hotels in France and Germany. Coming to the United States he started in at the Old Brunswick in New York City, and then at the Waldorf Astoria, New York City, then at Sherry's famous Cafe, New York City. He came to San Francisco to open the Hotel St. Francis in 1904.

PRESERVES, JELLIES AND PICKLES

For Jelly, select your fruit before it is too ripe if possible, as it is always a much better flavor.

It should be put on and brought to a heat as the juice can be much better extracted.

Have a bag made of flannel, in a funnel shape, to put the juice through. For straining it through the first time, use a wire sieve with a revolving wire to crush the fruit. Jelly should always be strained twice, and comes much clearer by allowing it to hang over night and drip.

Put on the juice and allow it to come to a boil, then put in the sugar, which should be first heated in the oven. Jelly should always boil rapidly in a pan with a very large bottom (copper is best) so that as much surface can be on the stove as possible. If it is desired to keep the color light, use a very little gelatine, so that it need not cook so long. From fifteen to twenty minutes is long enough for it to cook after it begins to boil and it should not stop till done.

Better success can be had by making it in small quantities.

After putting it in glasses set them in a hot sun till cold, then cover with melted paraffin.

If corn-starch be put in the juice before adding the sugar, it will make it clearer—two teaspoonfuls in two tablespoonfuls of water to three pints of juice.

A teaspoonful of sugar put upon the top of jelly in the glass prevents moulding. To prevent preserves from sugaring, add a little tartaric acid, when cooked.

Small stone jars are best for preserves. If glass jars are used they should be wrapped in paper to keep out the light.

Cider vinegar is best for pickles. If vinegar is too strong, dilute partly with water. All pickles should be tightly sealed to prevent air

14

reaching the vinegar, as this kills it. It should always be poured on hot as it comes to the first scald, never allowing it to boil. Never put up pickles in anything that has held any kind of grease, and never let them freeze.

If pickles are put into the brine, it should always be strong enough to bear an egg.

Use coarse salt in proportion of a heaping pint of salt to a gallon of water. Put pickles in bottles and seal while hot.

Put a slice of horse radish in each jar or bottle of pickles, this keeps the vinegar clear.

To one barrel of pickles add one-half bushel grape leaves while in the brine. This keeps them sound and firm.

LIST OF FRUIT IN PRESERVES

7½ pounds cherries
7½   "   sugar   } ....1 gallon preserves
14 pounds berries
14   "   sugar   } ....5 quarts jam

Two quarts of stemmed currants make two pints of juice, added to two pounds of sugar makes three tumblers of jelly.

Always wash strawberries before removing hulls, put in colander to drain. Always select strawberries for their flavor rather than their size.

STRAWBERRY PRESERVES

Prepare a small quantity at a time for best results. Have a kettle of syrup made of two pounds cane sugar and half a cup of water. Drop berries into it, cook rapidly for twenty minutes, do not stir fruit; remove any scum which may arise. Lift out and put in tumblers and when all are done, cook the syrup and juice to a jelly and fill up tumblers. Let stand till cold before covering.

BLACKBERRY JAM

4 quarts blackberries
2   "   fine cooked apples
4   "   cane sugar

Boil twenty-five to thirty minutes.

15

RASPBERRY OR LOGANBERRY JAM

To use one-third currants to two-thirds red raspberries is better than the berries alone. (Loganberries are acid enough.) Wash the fruit well and let it boil twenty minutes: Weigh the quantity, and to every pound of fruit, use three-quarters of a pound of sugar. Boil till, by taking some on a saucer to try it, no juice gathers about it. Put in small jars or glasses same as you would jelly.

CANNED STRAWBERRIES

Wash well before hulling and weigh and to each pound of berries allow one-quarter pound of cane sugar. Boil fifteen minutes, put in pint glass jars and seal while hot.

APPLE JELLY

Take ripe Bellefleur or any finely flavored cooking apples. Cut in quarters and remove the core. Drop in water as you cut them to prevent turning black. Add a little lemon juice to the water. When all are cut, drain off the water, and put apples in a preserving kettle (copper) and pour over them a little water. Let cook until soft, then strain through flannel bag, boil juice with an equal weight of sugar until it jells. Pour while hot in jelly glasses.

BLACKBERRY JUICE

Heat berries to a boiling point, mash and strain through flannel bag. Add an equal quantity of sugar to the juice. Boil hard for twenty-five minutes, then pour into glasses.

CURRANT JELLY

Wash and strip currants from the stems, and put them on to cook. Mash as they get hot. Let them boil twenty-five minutes, turn into jelly bag and let drip without squeezing. Measure juice and return it to kettle, after it has boiled about ten minutes add heated sugar, allowing a pound of sugar to a pint of juice. Cook until a little poured on a saucer, jells. Pour into moulds and seal when cold.

BRANDIED PEACHES

Take white sound peaches, rub with a crash towel to remove down, prick with a needle, drop in cold water, drain, put in kettle, cover with

cold water, add small piece of alum the size of a hazelnut. Place on fire and stir occasionally and as they float on top of the liquid, take out and place them in a pan of cold water. Drain and arrange in quart glass jars. Seal and put away in a cool place for two weeks, then drain off brandy into a kettle, and allow three pounds of sugar to each gallon of brandy. Stir well to melt sugar. Pour this over the peaches, seal hermetically and put away in a cool place.

CRANBERRY JELLY

To three quarts of cranberries, take two pounds of granulated cane sugar and one quart of water. Cook thoroughly and mash through a fine sieve. Return juice to the stove and cook fifteen minutes more. Pour into individual moulds.

CRAB APPLE MARMALADE AND JELLY

Take eight quarts of crab apples and add three quarts of water. Boil slowly for one hour, adding water that evaporates. Strain through flannel bag, and do not squeeze. Allow the same amount of sugar as juice. Boil for twenty minutes. Pour into glasses, seal when cold. Take remainder of apples, press through sieve, take equal parts cane sugar and pulp, cook until well done. Can be seasoned with lemon and cinnamon.

APRICOT MARMALADE

Remove stones and cut in halves some firm, ripe apricots. Add a few spoonfuls of water and cook until soft. Strain through sieve and add three-fourths of a pound of cane sugar to every pound of fruit. Crack as many stones as desired, and add the kernels to the fruit. Continue to stir and cook until it thickens, then pour immediately into hot glasses. Cover when perfectly cold. Peaches can be prepared the same way.

BRANDIED CHERRIES

Select some fine Queen Annie cherries, cut off about half the stems. Arrange the cherries in glass jars or bottles and pour over them the following syrup:

Melt two and one-half pounds granulated cane sugar with a very little water, being very careful not to let it

17

scorch. Take off fire and add half a vanilla bean. Then add slowly one gallon brandy, when cold pour over the cherries. Seal well and keep in a cool place.

PRESERVED CHERRIES

To each pound of stoned cherries allow one pound of granulated cane sugar, crack some of the stones and tie the kernels in a piece of gauze to be removed after the boiling, add the sugar to the cherries and let stand three hours before cooking. Then put them in a preserving kettle and boil and skim until the fruit is clear. Lift the cherries into jars and boil the syrup a little longer and pour over the fruit.

PRESERVED GAGE PLUMS

Use a pound of sugar to each pound of plums. Have the fruit clean and dry and prick all over with a needle to keep the skins from breaking. Melt the sugar with as little water as possible and when boiling add the plums, a layer at a time. Boil for a few minutes, lift out with a skimmer, and place singly on a dish to cool. Continue in this way until all the plums are done, then when the last layer is finished, return the first ones cooked to the kettle, boil until transparent. This time take out and arrange neatly in glass jars. Continue until each layer is finished. When all are done, pour the hot syrup over them. Seal up as usual.

QUINCE JELLY

To each pound of cut up quinces add a cup of water. Put in a kettle and stew until soft. Don't crush, put them in a jelly bag to drain. Add a pound of sugar to each pint of liquor. Let boil gently until sugar is dissolved then boil more quickly, pour into glasses and cover with paraffin when cold.

PRESERVED PEARS

Peel, half and remove core of Bartlett or Seckle pears, allow one pound of sugar to each pound of fruit. Put the sugar on to cook with a few spoonfuls of water. Stick a clove in each piece of fruit. Boil until thoroughly done. Put the fruit in glass jars, and cover with the syrup and seal. The juice and rind of one lemon to every five pounds of fruit can be used instead of cloves or both can be used.

PINEAPPLE PRESERVES

Pare and slice the pineapples, then weigh them. To every pound of fruit, take one pound of cane sugar, put a layer of slices in a stone jar, sprinkle over with sugar, and continue until fruit and sugar are used up. Let stand over night; take the apples out of the syrup, cook the syrup till it thickens, add the pineapples and boil fifteen minutes. Lift out the fruit from the syrup and let it cool, then put in jars and pour the syrup over. A very little ginger root boiled in the syrup improves it.

CANNED PEARS, PEACHES OR PLUMS

Twelve pounds of fruit and three pounds of sugar will fill six quart jars.

CITRON PRESERVES

Select sound fruit, pare it, divide into quarters, take out all seeds, and cut up in small pieces. Weigh it, to every pound of fruit, allow one-half pound of granulated cane sugar. Put the citron to cook until quite clear, drain through a colander, throw away the water it was cooked in; then put on the weighed sugar with a few spoonfuls of water to start it boiling. Let it boil until very clear, and before putting in the citron again, add to the syrup two large lemons sliced, and a small piece of ginger root; then add the citron and let all cook together about fifteen minutes. Fill the jars with citron, and pour over the hot syrup and seal up.

WATER MELON PRESERVES

Select one with a thick rind, cut in any shape desired, lay it in strong salt water for two or three days, then soak in clear water twenty-four hours, changing the water frequently; then put them in alum water for two hours to harden them. To every pound of fruit, use one pound of sugar. Make a syrup of the sugar and a few pieces of ginger root, and one lemon sliced thin. Take out the lemon and ginger after boiling a few minutes. Add the melon, boil until transparent. Lift carefully and place in glass jars, pouring the syrup over it.

19

SWEET PICKLED PEACHES

Take clingstone peaches and peel or rub the down off with a coarse crash towel. For eight pounds of fruit take four pounds of sugar, one quart of vinegar, one ounce stick cinnamon, and one ounce whole cloves. Boil sugar and vinegar with the cinnamon for two minutes; then put in the fruit a few at a time with one or two cloves stuck in each. When done, take out and place in jars and put in others to cook, until they have all been cooked. Reduce the syrup to one-half the original quantity and pour over the fruit; seal hot. This recipe can be used for plums and pears.

CANNED APPLES AND QUINCES

Pare and cut equal quantities of apples and quinces. First cook the quinces in sufficient water to cover them, till they are tender. Take them out and cook the apples in the same water. Put in a vessel a layer of quinces, then a layer of apples till all are used. Pour over them a syrup made of a half a pound of sugar to a pound of fruit and let stand over night. The next day boil for five minutes and seal in jars.

CANNED PEACHES

Pare the peaches, cut in half and lay in cold water till ready. Put on the stove a pound of sugar with three pints of water. Let boil to a syrup. Set the jars in a cloth in hot water. Fill the jars with the cold peaches, putting a generous layer of sugar between the peaches; when the jar is full of peaches, fill up with the hot syrup and seal immediately.

CANNED PEARS

Ten pounds of peeled, halved and cored pears, five pounds of granulated sugar, one sliced lemon, one teaspoonful ground cinnamon, a little grated nutmeg, a small piece of ginger root. Put the cinnamon and nutmeg loosely in a piece of gauze. Cook all together till the pears turn pink, then put in jars and seal hot.

TOMATO PRESERVES

Scald and peel carefully small pear-shaped tomatoes, half ripe, prick them with a needle to prevent them from bursting, and put their weight in sugar over them. Let them lie over night; then pour off the

liquid into a preserving kettle, and boil until it is a thick syrup. Clarify it with the white of an egg; add the tomatoes and boil until transparent. A small piece of ginger root or one lemon to a pound of fruit sliced very thin and cooked in the syrup improves it.

APPLE BUTTER

Three gallons of cooked apples and one quart of cider, five pounds brown sugar, several sticks cinnamon, boil down to about two gallons.

CALIFORNIA MARMALADE

One grape fruit, one orange, two lemons. Shave very thin, discard seeds only. Pack lightly into an earthen vessel and add enough water to just cover and let stand over night or twenty-four hours; then bring to a boil and let simmer for fifteen minutes; return to vessel and let stand for another twenty-four hours. Next day, measure and add equal quantities of sugar to fruit, return to stove and boil until it jells. Put up in jelly glasses.

GOOSEBERRY JAM

Weigh half ripe gooseberries and to eight pounds of fruit add one teacupful water. Boil until soft, add eight pounds of heated sugar and continue boiling until clear.

GRAPE JELLY

To every eight pounds of fruit, take one cup of water, bring to a boil and crush, strain through a jelly bag. Measure the juice, measure and set aside an equal quantity of granulated cane sugar; then boil the juice half an hour. Add the sugar heated and let boil about ten minutes longer.

SPICED VINEGAR FOR PICKLES

One gallon cider vinegar.
One pound brown sugar.
Two tablespoonfuls each of mustard seed, celery seed and salt.
One tablespoonful each of tumeric powder, black pepper and mace.
Two nutmegs grated.
Three onions.
One handful grated horseradish.

SPICED CHERRIES

Nine pounds of fruit.

Four pounds of sugar.

One pint malt or cider vinegar.

One-half ounce cinnamon bark.

One-half ounce whole cloves.

Make a syrup of the ingredients and let boil for a few minutes before putting in the fruit. Cook the fruit until the skins break; then take out the fruit and boil down until thick and pour over the fruit hot.

SPICED SWEET APPLES

Take equal parts of sugar and vinegar, add a dozen cloves and a stick of cinnamon bark; when boiling add sweet apples and cook until apples are tender.

SPICED TOMATOES

Take red and yellow pear-shaped tomatoes, prick with a needle to prevent bursting, sprinkle with salt, let stand over night. Pack neatly in glass jars, and cover with the following spiced vinegar:

One pint of cider or malt vinegar, one tablespoonful sugar and one tablespoonful of each of the following: cinnamon, cloves, allspice, black pepper. The spices should be ground. Bring to boiling point and pour over tomatoes. Seal up when cold.

PICKLED ARTICHOKES

Select small tender artichokes, trim bottoms, remove the hardest leaves; let stand in alum water until ready to use. When all are ready bring to boiling point and let cool slowly. When cold, arrange in glass jars and pour over them a liquid made as follows: To every gallon of vinegar take one teacup sugar, one cup salt, teaspoonful alum, one-quarter ounce cloves and black pepper. Bring to boiling point and seal while hot.

PICKLED ONIONS

Select very small white onions. Peel and boil them in equal portions of sweet milk and water for ten minutes. Drain well out in glass jars and pour scalding spiced vinegar over immediately. Use no allspice as it would darken them, and no sugar.

PICKLES

Take one hundred green cucumbers about two inches long or less; peel as many small white onions as desired; wash all and put into a stone jar, sprinkle plenty of table salt over them and toss about with the hands. Let stand twenty-four hours, drain off liquor, place pickles and onions in glass jars and cover with hot spiced vinegar, no sugar. Seal hot. A small red pepper added to each jar improves them.

GREEN TOMATO PICKLE

One peck of green tomatoes, one dozen large onions sliced very thin. Put in separate jars, sprinkle salt between the tomatoes and let stand a few hours. Pour boiling water over onions and let stand. Then squeeze them both out and arrange them in stone jars in alternate layers, sprinkling through them celery seed and mustard seed. Pour over this a quart of vinegar and a pint of sugar brought to a boil. It is ready for use when cold.

RIPE CUCUMBER SWEET PICKLE

Pare twelve large cucumbers and take out the pulp. Cut them in strips, take two pounds of sugar and one pint of vinegar, one-half ounce cinnamon and cloves. Boil together and skim. Then put in the cucumbers and let cook until tender. Take out, let liquor reduce and pour over the cucumbers and cover lightly.

NASTURTIONS

Take those that are small and green. Put them in salt and water, changing it twice in the course of a week. When you have done collecting them, turn off brine and cover with scalding vinegar with a little alum in it. Use in salads.

SWEET GRAPE JUICE

Take twenty pounds of Concord grapes, add three quarts of water, crushing the grapes in the water, and put them in a porcelain kettle. Stir them well until they reach boiling point, and let simmer fifteen or twenty minutes; then strain through a cloth and add three pounds of white sugar. When the sugar is dissolved, strain again through a

cloth. Heat it to boiling point again. Pour it into pint or quart bottles and seal instantly. Have the bottles hot and use only new corks. Dip the necks with corks in, into the hot sealing wax.

PRESERVED VIOLETS

One pound of large full bloom violets. Cut off stems. Boil one and a half pounds of granulated sugar until a little dropped in cold water makes a soft ball. Throw in the violets, remove the pan from fire for a moment, stir gently, return pan to the fire and boil up once, change immediately to another vessel. Let stand over night, next day drain them through a sieve, pour syrup back into a copper pan, add a cupful more of sugar, and cook again until it hardens in water. Put in the violets and change once more to the vessel and leave again over night. After this, drain off again, pour this syrup back into the pan, boil it for a few minutes and add the violets, removing the pan at once from the fire. Stir lightly until it begins to crystallize, then pour the whole on sheets of paper, shake and separate the flowers carefully with the hands, and when dry, pick them from the sugar; arrange on a grating and leave to get cold.

CANNED MINCE MEAT

Three pounds of boiled beef, one pound of beef suet, three pounds of brown sugar, one-half peck apples, two pounds raisins, one pound currants, one pound citron, one nutmeg, grated, one tablespoonful mace, powdered, allspice and cinnamon to suit the taste. Chop the meat, suet and apples fine, then put them together with the seasoning. Slice the citron fine. Pour on enough boiled cider to make a thick batter of it. Heat it thoroughly and put into one quart glass jars. Seal while hot, and put away in a cool, dark place.

TO CAN PUMPKIN OR SQUASH

Cut squash or pumpkin in little squares, peel and put on to cook until soft. No seasoning. Mash through a fruit press, have ready one quart glass jars, hot. Fill them with the squash or pumpkin, seal tight, and keep in a cool dark place.

TO PRESERVE LIMES

Remove the cores from the limes (a small tin tube comes for this purpose), cover with salted water, a large handful of salt to a gallon of water. Let soak for four or five hours. Drain off the salt water,

throw the limes into boiling water. As soon as soft, take them out one by one, drop them into cold water. Change this water several times.

To turn them green again, put two gallons of water in an upturned copper pan. Add two large handfuls of cooking salt, one cup of vinegar and several handfuls of fresh spinach. Stand this kettle on the fire and let boil for a few minutes, drain the limes and throw into the boiling kettle, boil up several times. Take the basin from the fire. Let stand until cold, when they will have resumed their natural color; drain off the liquid and let the limes soak in fresh water for about fourteen hours, changing the water frequently. Prepare a fifteen degree syrup. When boiling, drain the limes and throw them into this, boil up and then put in a vessel and leave for twelve hours. The following day, pour off the syrup and boil it to sixteen degrees and pour it once more over the limes, leaving it for twelve hours; drain the syrup again, boil until it reaches twenty degrees. Pour it over the limes and leave for twelve hours longer, repeating this process every twelve hours until the syrup reaches thirty-two degrees; then pour it back into the kettle. When boiling, throw in the limes and boil for two minutes; put into small stone jars, and when cool, seal hermetically.

JELLIED CHERRIES

To three pounds of stoned sour cherries, take one pound of currant juice, and a handful of crushed kernels, tied up in a gauze bag, so they can be removed when the fruit is cooked. Put the cherries in a copper pan on a slow fire and reduce to about half, then add three pounds of granulated cane sugar and the pound of currant juice in which the kernels have been steeped. Continue to boil steadily until a little tried on a saucer will not spread. Now add half a gill of kirsch wasser (cherry brandy), put at once into jelly glasses. Place in a cool place, and when cold, cover with paraffin and put on the tin covers.

BLACKBERRY CORDIAL FOR MEDICINAL PURPOSES

Heat and strain ripe blackberries and to one pint of juice add one pound of granulated sugar, one-fourth ounce of powdered cinnamon, one-fourth ounce of mace, one teaspoonful of cloves. Boil all together for twenty minutes, strain the liquid and to each pint, add a gill of French brandy. · Put away in small bottles.

CANDIED LEMON OR ORANGE PEEL

Take a sufficient quantity of lemon or orange peels. Put on the fire with enough water to cover. Boil until soft to the touch, and throw into cold water; leave to soak for twenty-four hours, changing the water often. Drain, put into a stone jar, cover with a fifteen degree syrup, boiling. Let stand twelve hours, drain off the syrup boil it up to eighteen degrees, then pour it again over the peels, leaving them to steep for twelve hours. Repeat this operation six or seven times, gradually increasing the strength of the syrup until it reaches thirty-two degrees. The last time prepare a fresh thirty-two degree syrup. Drain the fruits from the syrup they are in and add them to the fresh boiling syrup—boil up once. Remove from fire, lay them in stone jars or pots, covered with the syrup and seal when cold.

FIG JAM

Take large firm figs, remove hard stems, cut in quarters. For each pound of figs take half a pound of sugar, dissolved in a little water. Boil this up once or twice, then add the figs and boil steadily until the marmalade coats the spoon and drops from it in beads; then pour into hot jelly glasses.

VANILLA BRANDY

Cut up vanilla beans very fine, pound in a mortar with a pestle, put in bottles and cover with strong brandy. This is much better than ordinary vanilla.

ORANGE OR LEMON BRANDY FOR FLAVORING

Take the very thin yellow outside of oranges or lemons, the white is not good. Brush with a little granulated sugar. Put in a bottle and cover with strong brandy. In this same way can be prepared and kept for use the kernels of cherries, also plum, apricot and peach stones, pounding them slightly before putting them in the brandy.

GLACED FRUITS

Be very particular in selecting the fruit. Cherries should be large and not quite ripe, firm and without blemishes, stones removed. Apricots medium sized and firm, remove stones without making too

large an opening and should be almost green. Peaches should be the same as apricots, pears should be peeled, leaving stems, and figs must be green. Strawberries must be very green, but full grown. Wash and dry well, leaving the stems in. Nectarines should be green and stones removed. Any hard green plums may be used, but leave their stones in. To candy pineapple, cut in thick slices, removing core and any brown outside spots. All fruits must be first washed and thoroughly dried before being prepared. It is well to make a new syrup for each kind of fruit. To make the syrup take two pounds granulated cane sugar and two gills of water and boil together for eight minutes. Have the fruit handy on a platter and lay each piece into the syrup. Do not pour into syrup or allow syrup to stop boiling. Wait a few seconds between each piece so the syrup can boil up well over the fruit. Then remove piece by piece in the order placed in kettle. Do not under any circumstances use a fork either for lifting or to test fruit. A silver spoon or an aluminum skimmer should always be used. Place the fruit on a thick piece of wax paper. Put in a cool place. The next day, repeat this process, adding the fruit as before. Allow to boil hard for a minute and remove as before. It takes about eight days for the fruit to absorb enough sugar and not to get mushy. That is why it is not allowed to cook for a continuous length of time. When finished, line a broad, shallow stone jar with waxed paper. Lay in piece by piece, not allowing them to touch each other. Put waxed paper between the layers and cover closely.

BAKED PEARS FOR CANNING

Wash as many ripe, firm, unspecked pears as will fill a baking pan. Pour boiling water over to almost fill the pan. Sweeten as though for immediate use. While the pears are baking, baste frequently and turn over and around to brown lightly, and evenly. Add a few cloves and a little stick cinnamon. Have glass jars as hot as for canning and when the pears are very tender, almost candied, pack in the jars; have juice cover the fruit. Seal while hot. Should the water evaporate very much, add more, little by little, until the syrup is enough to cover the pears when in the jars.

RASPBERRY JUICE

Mash clean ripe berries to a pulp, let stand overnight. Next morning strain through a jelly bag and to each pint of juice, add one

cupful of granulated cane sugar. Boil three minutes and seal hermetically in bottles, while hot. This recipe will answer for any berries or fruit. A good substitute for brandy or wine for puddings and sauces, also makes a delicious drink when added to a glass of ice water.

BOILED CIDER

To be used in Mince Pies, fruit cakes, etc., about a gill to a quart of mince meat or cake dough. Five quarts of sweet cider newly made and before fermentation has set in, place on the fire in a granite kettle. Boil slowly until reduced to one quart. Seal while hot.

MACEDOINE WATER ICE

Two pounds of sugar, three quarts of water, six lemons. Dissolve the sugar in the water, then add the grated yellow rind of two-thirds, the juice of six lemons, strain and freeze. When frozen add one quart of different kinds of fruits, such as small grapes, stoned cherries, apricots, strawberries and pineapple cut small. The fruits should be soaked in a strong kirsch syrup before using, which will prevent them from freezing too solid.

NORMANDY WATER ICE

Two pounds of sugar, three quarts of water, six lemons. Dissolve the sugar in the water, and then add the grated yellow rind of two lemons and the juice of the lemons and one quart of crab apple pulp and one gill of cognac. Freeze.

SORBET A EAU DE VIE DE DANTZIG

One pound of sugar, three pints of water, two lemons and one orange juice, two whites of eggs beaten with one gill of maraschino; freeze and serve in Sorbet glasses with Eau de Vie de Dantzig on top. Put the Eau de Vie de Dantzig at last moment so that the silver leaves will show.

SORBET PARLERMENTAIN

Two pounds of sugar, two quarts of water, six oranges, two lemons, dissolve the sugar with the water, infuse the grated rind of one orange and also the juice of the oranges and lemon, two yolks of eggs and two whites of eggs beaten with a small glass of curacao. Freeze and serve.

VICTOR HIRTZLER
CHEF DE CUISINE
HOTEL
ST. FRANCIS
San Francisco, Cal.

Mr. Hirtzler was born in Strasbourg, Alsace, Germany, and learned his profession under Emile Feypell in Strasbourg who is considered one of the finest Chefs in France. Mr. Hirtzler has been in the best hotels in France and Germany. Coming to the United States he started in at the Old Brunswick in New York City, and then at the Waldorf Astoria, New York City, then at Sherry's famous Cafe, New York City. He came to San Francisco to open the Hotel St. Francis in 1904.

VICTORIA PUNCH

Two pounds of sugar, two quarts of water and the juice of six oranges mixed altogether, and then add a small glass of rum, small

29

glass of Kirsch and a glass of Sautern. Freeze, and add the meringue of three whites of eggs and one-half pound of sugar. Serve in glasses.

BURGUNDY PUNCH

Two pounds of sugar, two quarts of water, rind of one and juice of six lemons and one piece of cinnamon stick. Let it stand for about two hours. Freeze and after being frozen add one pint of claret and a small glass of cognac and a drop of red coloring.

CARAMEL ICE CREAM

Boil one and one-half pounds of sugar with one pint water until little brown, stir two quarts of milk into the sugar and let boil until dissolved. Meanwhile mix one pint of milk with eight yolks of eggs and add the boiling milk stirring gradually until well mixed. Remove from fire, add one quart of cream and freeze.

BANANA ICE CREAM

One gallon of milk, twenty yolks and ten whole eggs, two pounds of sugar, mix the yolks of eggs with sugar and then boil the milk and pour it over the eggs; mix and cook until a little creamy, add the pulp of one dozen bananas and a few drops of banana extract.

FRESH RASPBERRY PUNCH

One pint of raspberry juice, fresh.

One pint of water.

One pound sugar and juice of two lemons.

Freeze and before serving, add four whites of eggs well beaten.

BISCUIT GLACE ST. FRANCIS

Four yolks of eggs, two ounces sugar,

One-fourth vanilla beans or essence,

One pint whipped cream.

Mix the sugar with the yolks and vanilla and cook for a few minutes, moving all the time with a whip. Take off the stove and beat until cold, then add the whipped cream. Fill up some fancy paper boxes and freeze. When frozen, decorate the top with strawberry and pistache ice cream and serve.

THEIR ICES, CREAMS AND SWEETS

CHAS. A. FREY
CHEF
HOTEL
ALEXANDRIA
Los Angeles, Cal.

Mr. Frey was first at the Hotel von Konig von England in Munster; later at the Dom Hotel, Cologne; Continental Hotel, Paris; with the North German Lloyd and Hamburg-American Steamship Lines and Hotel Bellevue-Stratford, Philadelphia.

STRAWBERRY MOUSSE

Whip one pint of heavy cream to a froth. Add two and a half ounces of powdered sugar. Dissolve three-quarters of an ounce of gelatine in a little warm water and strain it to the cream, beating the same rapidly. Then add one-quarter pint crushed strawberries. Fill in moulds and set in shaved ice with salt until it commences to freeze. Then dip the mould in warm water and remove the contents on a cold dish. Decorate with whipped cream and fresh strawberries.

ICED TEA

Place one ounce of selected tea in a teapot, large enough to hold four glasses of iced tea. Fill full of boiling water, let stand for a second, or, if desired very strong, a little longer. Strain in an earthen jar, placed in ice and let get cold. Then pour in glasses and serve with pieces of ice and fine granulated sugar and slices of lemon.

ICE CREAM AND ICES

NOTICE: In making ice cream and water ices all sugar which is used for the same should be boiled into a syrup and used accordingly, scaled by a special sugar scaler in degrees. The following recipes are scaled with a Beaume sugar scale wherever it is possible.

CAFE PARFAIT ALEXANDRIA

Make a very strong coffee and pour over one pound of cube sugar. Dissolve the same over a slow fire but do not let it boil until it reaches twenty-eight degrees.

Beat eight yolks of eggs in a kettle which is placed in a hot water bath, then add the above coffee syrup little by little. Remove the kettle with its contents out of the hot water in shaved ice. Keep on beating same until very cold, then add one pint of whipped cream, mix well, then place the same in cold parfait glasses and place in freezer until frozen solid, serving in same glasses.

31

ICE CREAM YOKOHOMA

Work one pound of almond paste with one pint of milk and pass through a fine sieve. Then beat in a kettle twelve ounces of sugar with nine yolks of eggs, then add one quart of boiling cream, one-fourth vanilla bean and one tablespoonful of tea leaves. Mix the same well on a slow fire and just before it starts to boil remove the same from fire and add the above described almond milk. Then strain the whole through a tamy (heavy cheese cloth), let get cold and freeze in a freezer. When frozen serve in special out of pulled sugar prepared butterfly designs.

CHOCOLATE MOUSSE ANNA HELD

Melt one-half pound chocolate in one pint of hot water, one-half vanilla bean; let boil a minute, add one pint of syrup, at twenty-eight degrees and strain the same, place in ice and let get very cold.

Beat in a kettle, one quart of whipping cream, add the above dissolved chocolate and mix the same. Then place the same in moulds and freeze. When frozen serve in special made out of red pulled sugar prepared rose designs and decorate on top with whipped cream and fresh strawberries.

ICE CREAM AL'IMPERATRICE

Boil two ounces of rice in water for five minutes, then remove the water and add one and a half pints of milk, one-half vanilla bean and boil very well. Then pass through a fine sieve and set on ice to cool.

Beat in a kettle, six yolks of eggs with one-half pound of sugar, add a quart of boiling cream and let come to boil, but not boiling, then add the above described mixture and let get cold. Then freeze in a freezer. When frozen mix in some maraschino soaked candied fruit which is cut in dice such as pineapple and cherries.

ORANGE ICE COVINA

Grate the rind of two dozen oranges carefully. Add four pounds of granulated sugar, let stand for one hour, then add one gallon of water and the juice of the grated oranges. Let stand until all sugar is dissolved, then strain and add two whites of egg and freeze. When frozen cut a thin layer of pound cake round, place on these thin sliced oranges and on top of these place the orange ice in shape of a pyramid.

BAVAROIS OF APRICOTS

Dissolve one and one-fourth ounces of good gelatine in one pint of lukewarm water. Add one-half pound sugar. Let stand for ten minutes and strain. Then add one pint of apricot pulp made of fresh apricots by removing skin and pits and passed through a fine sieve Add two ounces Kirschwasser.

Beat in a kettle one pint of whipping cream. When stiff mix with the above and place in moulds, then set in refrigerator until firm. Then remove the mould by dipping in warm water. Place the Bavarois on a special cold dish and garnish with whipped cream and brandied apricots.

Charles A. Frey

SHERBET A' LA'DUSE

Boil one quart of water with one pound granulated sugar for twenty minutes. Cool, add the juice of six lemons, three oranges and whites of six eggs. Mix thoroughly and strain through a cheese cloth and freeze. After freezing add one pony of anisette, one pony maraschino and one pony of sloe gin. Mix thoroughly. Set aside for one hour. Serve with whipped cream.

BOMBE TRIUNWIR

Prepare four ounces of marrons, glace and four ounces of Moutarde De Cremona. Chop very fine. Work into a still paste with a little kummel. Line four bombe molds with water ice. Place in center of the ice cream one spoonful of the paste. Cover tight with ice cream and close the mold very tight, pack in ice and salt for two hours. When ready to serve, dip into hot water, remove the mould and serve on a lace doily.

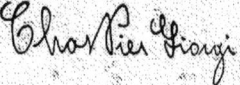

CHARLES
PIER GIORGI
CHEF DE CUISINE
HOTEL ALCAZAR
St. Augustine, Fla.

Prior to coming to the Hotel Alcazar, Mr. Giorgi was at the Hotel Walton and the Gilsey House, New York City; the Bay Shore House at City Island, N.Y.; the Hollywood Hotel at West End, N.J., and at the Hotel Kittatinny at Delaware Water Gap Pa.

G. MILHAU
CHEF DE CUISINE
TAIT-ZINKAND
CAFE
San Francisco, Cal.

Mr. Milhau learned his trade at the Cafe Boudoul at Marseilles, France. Following this he was Chef at the Grand Hotel De la Paix at Florence, Italy., Coming to this country he was at the Union Club, Boston, the Tour-raine Hotel, Boston, the Metropolitan Club and at the St. Regis Hotel, New York City. He came west with Mr. Emile Bailly to open the Fairmont Hotel in San Francisco.

TARTELLETTES CALIFORNIA

Shape your moulds with short paste, the cook, put in a half peach and decorate aroun with cherries and strawberries. Cover the moul with a thick raspberry syrup flavored wit maraschino.

BOMBE NELUSKO

Line the mould with pralines ice crean fill the inside with mousse of chocolate an freeze.

GLACE PRALINES

Vanilla ice cream to which has been adde the following: nine ounces sugar and a sixth a pint of water, cook the sugar to breakir point and add two ounces of browned almon which have been baked in an oven; mix we over a fire to give it a golden color. Cool o and chop up very fine; add to ice cream.

CHAMPAGNE SHERBET

For one quart of sherbet take as follow The juice of three lemons and half of one orang half a pint of champagne, sweeten to seventee or eighteen degrees by the syrup scale. Prepar freezer in the usual way and work the sherb with a wooden spatula until it gets solid, the add three whites of egg made into an Italian meringue. Serve i champagne glasses.

MOUSSE OF CHOCOLATE

Mix ten yolks of eggs with half a pint of syrup at twenty-eigl degrees, pass through sieve into a china cup and put on to cook i Bain Marie. When the mixture begins to thicken take out of wat and set aside to cool; whip up the mixture meanwhile like you woul for Genoise cake, add about three-quarters of a quart of whipped crea and mix well.

34

PUNCH A L'IMPERIALE

One pint of strong infused tea, one gill of pineapple juice, the juice of two lemons, one-quarter gill of brandy, one-quarter gill benedictine, six ounces of sugar, two whites of eggs, the rind of one orange. Put sugar and all liquids excepting the liquor in a pan, heat without boiling and strain—when cold add the whites of eggs and freeze, then mix in the liquor. Serve in glasses—decorate the top with oranges and cherries.

ADRIAN DELVAUX
CHEF DE CUISINE
HOTEL BALTIMORE
Kansas City, Mo.
Mr. Delvaux started in at the Grand Hotel in Rheims, France, and thence to the Bristol Hotel in Paris. In this country, at the Chicago Club, Hotel Congress and Annex, Chicago and at the Auditorium Hotel, Chicago. He has been at the Hotel Baltimore for five years, where he has made the Baltimore famous for its cuisine.

BALTIMORE SHERBET

Grate two pineapples and mix with two quarts of water and one pint of sugar. Add the juice of two lemons and the beaten whites of four eggs. Place in a freezer and freeze and garnish with six strawberries on each dish.

GRAPE FRUIT ICE

Pour into a vessel some syrup made with two and a quarter pounds of sugar and one pint of water cooked together. When cool, add juice of two good sized grape fruit, strain and freeze.

ICE CREAM A LA BALTIMORE

Place in a thin basin, six ounces sugar, four yolks of eggs, half a lemon peel and dilute with one and a half pints of boiling cream. Thicken the preparation on the fire, stirring well. When done, strain through a sieve into vessel and stir until cool. Then freeze same. After frozen hard, mix one cupful of raspberry syrup and then serve with a small amount of whipped cream on top.

PUNCH VICTORIA

One pint of water, two whites of eggs, six ounces sugar, juice of two lemons, rind of one orange, the juice of two, half a gill southern wine, a little stick cinnamon and some brandied peaches chopped very

fine. Put sugar, water, lemon juice, the orange rind and juice of two oranges and stick cinnamon in a pan, heat without boiling and strain. When cold, put in the whites and freeze. When nearly frozen, mix in the fine chopped brandied peaches, let it freeze more, then mix in the liquor. Serve with a nice slice of peach and a cherry on top.

COUPE NANETTE

Fill half full the coupe glass of fresh fruit salad. Slice bananas a quarter inch thick around the glass on surface of the fruit salad, flavor with benedictine. Use vanilla and pistachio on top of the fruit with a spoon of strawberry ice cream on top of the vanilla and pistachio ornament with fresh fruit.

GLACE A L'HARANAISE

Six yolks of eggs, four ounces sugar, one pint whipped cream, two ounces chopped macaroons, half a pint chopped pineapple, quarter of a pint fresh strawberries, one gill of maraschino. Put the yolks in a basin, add the sugar and beat to a sponge, then add the cream and continue to stir over the fire until nearly boiling, strain when cold, freeze. When nearly done, mix in the chopped macaroons, straw-berries and pineapple. When ready, mix the maraschino and whipped cream and freeze some more.

A Delvaux

LOUIS THEIN
FORMERLY
CHEF DE CUISINE
HOTEL UTAH
Salt Lake City, Utah.
Mr. Thein has been with some of the best Hotels and Cafes in America.

STRAWBERRY ICE CREAM

Place two quarts fresh strawberries in a bowl, six egg yolks, eight ounces powdered sugar, two pints cream, mix well. Place the contents in small ice cream freezer; place the freezer in a tub. See that the freezer is completely buried in cracked ice mixed with rock salt, then briskly freeze for thirty minutes, seeing that the ice cream is thoroughly firm. Dress the ice cream on a dish and send to the table.

TUTTI FRUTTI ICE CREAM

Prepare and finish a vanilla ice cream. Chop very fine six candied cherries, pears, apricots, candied prunes, figs, one ounce angelica candied

marrons, place all in a bowl, season, little Kirsch, rum, maraschino; mix well. Then add the vanilla ice cream and mix well with a wooden spoon for two minutes. Carefully fill a quart brick ice cream mould with the cream. Cover both sides with lightly buttered paper, then cover it and bury the mould in broken ice and rock salt. Let freeze for one hour, unmould on a cold dish with a folded napkin and send to the table.

BAKED ALASKA

Place three lady fingers on a plate. Put ice cream on top. Beat six egg whites until hard. Decorate the top with same and place in hot oven for two seconds and serve.

Louis Thein

E. C. PERAULT
CHEF DE CUISINE
PLANTERS HOTEL
St. Louis, Mo.

Mr. Perault was born in Lyon, France. On coming to this country was at the Mercantile and University Clubs, St. Louis, Grand Hotel Mackinac, Mackinac, Mich.; the Eastman Hotel, Hot Springs; and the Antlers, Colorado Springs.

PUNCH MOSCOWITE

Take four pounds granulated sugar, one gallon black tea (not too strong), add one pint rum, and one pint kirschwasser, one grated orange, the juice of fourteen lemons, and the white of two eggs and then freeze. It is very appropriate to serve this punch in cocktail glasses, decorated on top with fresh fruit.

SORBET AUX PECHES

Take one gallon of water, three quarts fresh crushed peaches, five pounds sugar, the juice of eight lemons, add one ounce of fine cut peach nuts, this will give the sherbet a delicious flavor; this can be served in half orange peel and decorated with peaches.

GRANITE AUX ANNANAS

Take four pounds sugar, one gallon of water, the juice of twelve lemons, three quarts fine grated pineapple, the white of one egg, freeze well. Serve in a fancy glass. Cut fresh pineapple in dices and display on top of ice.

Edmond Perault

HENRI BOUTROUE
CHEF DE CUISINE
HOTEL
SHELBOURNE
Dublin, Ireland

Mr. Boutroue was formerly with the Clifton Down Hotel at Bristol, England, the Queen's Hotel at Leeds, England, the Savoy Hotel in London; the Laugham, London, also the Hotel Metropole, London.

BOMBE TOGO

Vanilla ice cream, powdered macaroons and candied cherries cut in dice. Serve Bombe with garniture of preserved cherries and syrup of same (reduce the latter to half), a little Bar-le-duc arrowroot; put the cherries in syrup and let freeze.

Henri Boutroue

JOHN CHIAPPANO
CHEF DE CUISINE
AUDITORIUM
HOTEL
Chicago, Ill.

Mr. Chiappano has been with some of the finest Hotels in this country and Europe.

PEACHES A LA TORINESE

Preserved peaches, stuffed with hazelnut ice cream. Serve on sponge cake with wine jelly.

John Chiappano

CESAR OBRECHT
CHEF DE CUISINE
GRAND HOTEL
DE L'EUROPE
Lucerne, Switzerland
also
PALACE HOTEL
LTD.
Murren, Switzerland
Mr. Obrecht, prior
to holding his present
position, was at the
Grand Savoy Hotel at
Florence, at the Grand
Hotel and Kurhaus, at
St. Blasien; the Grand
Hotel de Thouwe at
Thouwe, the Grand
Hotel Krasnapolsky at
Amsterdam, the Grand
Hotel de Salines at
Reinfelden and the
Grand Hotel Waldhaus
at Vulpera.

MOUSSE DAME BLANCHE

(White Dame Mousse)

Proportions three yolks of eggs, half a pint of syrup twenty-eight degrees, vanilla, one pint of whipped cream. Mix yolks and syrup and strain. Set to cook in a vessel immersed in boiling water. Flavor with the vanilla and beat with fork from time to time. When it commences to thicken, and is sufficiently consistent, put into cold vessel and beat until completely cooled down. It ought to get double its size. Add then the whipped cream, put into a mould and let stand on salted ice one and a half hours.

César Obrecht

· ERNEST
OTZENBERGER
CHEF DE CUISINE
HOTEL DENNIS
Atlantic City, N.J.
Mr. Otzenberger was
formerly Chef for G.
W. Vanderbilt in Paris,
London and New York.

MOUSSE A LA VANDERBILT

Strawberries, raspberries, apricots, peaches, pineapple, etc., to be used. A quart of cream must be whipped till very light. Drain it on a sieve and then transfer it to a bowl. Add a pound of Pineapple puree and one pound of sugar, mixing both together with a little vanilla and a gill of Kirsch. Whip the preparation in a tin basin on ice for ten minutes to have the cream and pulp assimilate well together. Coat the inside of a high dome mold with virgin strawberry cream; fill the center quite full with the preparation and close the mold. Pack in ice for one hour for each quart. Serve in mold on a napkin, with small iced cakes.

VIRGIN STRAWBERRY CREAM

To be made with one pint of the pulp of strawberry, one pint of cream, one gill of syrup and a little vanilla bean, ten ounces sugar. Strain through a very fine sieve and freeze.

WALTER JURENZ
CHEF DE CUISINE
HOTEL GALVEZ
Gàlveston, Tex.

Mr. Jurenz, prior to coming to this country, was with some of the finest hotels in Italy, France and England. He was Chef to Count Waldersee and his staff to China, the Red Lion Hotel at Henley on the Thames, England, Royal Crown Hotel, the Belgravia Hotel, and the Vienna Cafe, London, England. In this country, at Hotel La Salle, Hotel Congress and Annex, Chicago, and the Chicago Yacht Club.

FRENCH APPLE TARTE

Use tarte dough, spread out thin in pie pan, fill up with raw sliced apples, granulated sugar, powdered cinnamon, sprinkle over some lemon juice and a few currants, then make a screen of dough on top and fill empty spaces between the dough with jelly and bake like any other pie.

STARS AND STRIPES BANNER PUNCH

Use a sherbet with any cordial flavoring, and put into a fancy punch glass, then stick an American flag on top and serve it.

OLD FASHIONED COFFEE PARFAIT

Mix together in a bowl, half and half chocolate ice cream and whipped cream and shredded ice, then fill this into high stem glasses and garnish with whipped cream with a cherry on top.

Walter Jurenz

41

EMILE BAILLY,
CHEF DE CUISINE
HOTEL ST. REGIS
New York City, N.Y.
Mr. Bailly prior to
coming to this country
served in the very best
hotels in Europe. He
left the Grand Hotel
of Monte Carlo, France,
ten years ago, to come
to New York and open
the St. Regis.

PONCIRE PRINTANIERE

Two poncires split in two. Take out the interior. Then prepare the following fruits: apple, pineapple, pear, grape and the inside part of the poncire. Cut all in dice. Mix with one spoon of maraschino, one teaspoon kirsch, a little powdered sugar, stuff the empty poncire with the fruit compote. Decorate to your taste with strawberry, cherries or any kind of fruit of red color. Serve in cup glass on ice.

CREAM GLACE BONNE MAMA

Whip very firm three quarters of a pint of double cream, then four ounces of powdered sugar with vanilla. Four macaroons in crumbs, soak in kirsch and maraschino, also four chestnuts glaced and have all these ingredients well mixed. Take a one pint ice cream bombe mould and fill with the before mentioned mixture and let freeze for an hour and a half. Dip the mould in warm water and turn the ice cream out of the mould on a dish with a napkin and decorate with maraschino cherries and the rest of the whipped cream and serve.

MERINGUES GLACE

Regular meringue shells filled with different ice creams; top garnished with fancy whipped cream, angelica and candied cherries as decoration.

Emile Bailly

LUCIEN FUSIER
CHEF DE CUISINE
GRAND HOTEL
METROPOLE
Interlaken, Switzerland

Mr. Fusier was for-
merly at the Shep-
heard's Hotel at Cairo,
the Grand Hotel du
Louvre at Menton,
France, Hotel Schwei-
zerhof at Interlaken,
Switzerland; Tunisia
Palace, Tunis; the
Yongfraublick Hotel at
Interlaken, Switzerland,
and at the Cap Hotel,
Bordighera, Portugal.

BOMBE EXCELSIOR

Take a half pint of apricot pulp, strained
through a fine sieve, one-fourth pint of water,
sugar until it attains twenty degrees and let
freeze. Coat the sides of a bombe mould with
this mixture and fill interior with a maraschino
moss mixed with pieces of macaroons dipped in
maraschino. For the mousse: Break four yolks
of eggs in a dish, one-fourth pint of twenty-eight
degree syrup, mix the while and thicken in a
vessel submerged in another one filled with warm
water. Let cool by beating it. Add half pint of
whipped cream, one glass of maraschino and the
macaroons. Close the mould and let freeze for
one and a half hours.

Lucien Fusier.

43

EDWARD
R. J. FISCHEL
STEWARD
HOTEL PIEDMONT
Atlanta, Ga.

Mr. Fischel was apprenticed under the famous Jean Marie Laporte and has been at the following hotels: Hoffman House, New York City, Cafe Savarin, N. Delmonico and the Congress and Annex, Chicago.

SHERBET PARFAIT D'AMOUR

Prepare one quart of water, twelve ounces of sugar and six lemons; make sugar and water into a syrup, let infuse with the grated rind of six lemons, add the juice of the lemons and strain. Beat the white of two eggs and pour into syrup while warm, adding a teaspoonful of vanilla flavoring extract and freeze. Add while freezing, a wine glass of orange juice and half a wine glass of strawberry juice and just before serving pour into it half a wine glass of rum and a tablespoon of kirschwasser. Serve in Sherbet glasses.

BAVAROISE EN BELLEVUE

Line the mold with clear wine jelly; decorate the bottom with a star or any other fancy design of Angelica and cherries. Fasten the fruit to the sides by dipping in some jelly. When the lining is set fill with the following Bavarian cream:

Half a pint of plain cream; half a pint of double cream; the yolk of five eggs; four ounces sugar, one ounce of leaf gelatine and vanilla flavor.

Soak the gelatine in a little cold water; beat the double cream firm and let drain on a sieve. Put the yolks, sugar and plain cream on the fire, stir until it thickens but do not let boil. Take off, stir in the gelatine; strain and add the flavor. Stir on ice until it begins to set then mix with the whipped cream. Fill into the cold form and set on ice until wanted.

**EMILE
BURGERMEISTER**
CHEF DE CUISINE
HOTEL FAIRMONT
San Francisco, Cal.

Mr. Burgermeister was assistant to Mr. Emile Bailly, the well known Chef of the St. Regis, New York City, and worked with him at the Grand Hotel at Monte Carlo, France; at the Hotel Adlon, Berlin, Germany; the Frankfurter-hof, at Frankfurt, Germany, and the Pavilion Royal at Paris. He worked under Wm. A. Escoffier at the famous Ritz-Carlton Hotel in London, to learn the wonderful Ritz-Carlton organization.

PINEAPPLE COUPE AU KIRSCH

Preserved pineapple cut in dice, not too large, flavor with Kirschwasser, and fill up the glass with lemon water ice with whipped cream on top.

MARQUISE CALIFORNIA

Orange water ice, flavored with cognac, mixed with meringue (beaten white of egg and sugar filled in orange in imitation of stems and leaves in sugar).

STRAWBERRY ROMANOFF

Ripe nice strawberries, cooled off in glass bowl on ice, pour some Chartreuse, with good whipped cream on top, flavor with vanilla and serve, very cold.

45

LUCIEN RAYMOND
CHEF DE CUISINE
**HOTEL CONGRESS
AND ANNEX**
Chicago, Ill.

Prior to coming to this country, Mr. Raymond was at the Ritz Hotel in Paris, the Ritz Hotel in London, and the Trianon Palace at Versailles, France. On coming to this country he was at the famous Ritz-Carlton, New York.

POIRE MARY GARDEN

(Pears, Mary Garden)

Dress pears on a canopy of vanilla ice cream and cover pears with a strawberry mousse and fine chopped almonds.

NEIGE AU CLIQUOT

(Fruit Snow with Cliquot Champagne)

Lemon water ice with Cliquot Champagne, served in Flute Champagne Glasses.

PEACHES GLACES WILHELMINE

(Frozen Peaches Wilhelmine)

Peaches on a canopy of Tangarine Water Ice covered with a praline and velvet of spun sugar.

COUPE CZARINE

Lemon ice with kummel and whipped cream on top.

L. Raymond

**BEN E.
DUPAQUIER**
CHEF DE CUISINE
**HOTEL
ARLINGTON**
Santa Barbara, Cal.

Mr. Dupaquier's first position was in The Pendennis Club, of Louisville, Ky. Later at the Gault House, Louisville, the Missouri Athletic Club, the Mercantile Club and the New Jefferson Hotel of St. Louis; the Jonathan Club and the California Club, Los Angeles and the Hotel Maryland, Pasadena, Cal.

MARRON ICE CREAM

Prepare a vanilla ice cream. Finely chop two ounces candied marrons and add to the ice cream in the freezer with two tablespoons maraschino. Mix well and serve.

VANILLA ICE CREAM (1 quart)

Six yolks eggs, eight ounces powdered sugar, one pint fresh milk and one stick vanilla. Place the egg yolks and sugar in a small saucepan and mix thoroughly with a wooden spoon for five minutes.

Place the cream, milk and vanilla into another small saucepan and let come to a boil; then immediately pour it into the eggs and sugar, little by little, carefully mixing with the wooden spoon while heating, for five minutes, but under no circumstances allowing it to boil. Remove from the fire, pour it into a bowl and allow it to thoroughly cool off. Remove the vanilla and strain the cream through a Chinese strainer into a small ice cream freezer. Place the freezer in a tub, see that the freezer is completely buried in cracked ice, mixed with rock salt, then briskly freeze for thirty minutes; see that the ice cream is thoroughly firm.

Ben E. Dupaquier

MERINGUES PANACHEES

Four whites of eggs, well beaten, half a pound powdered sugar, put in pastry bag and form on piece of paper which rests on a sugar covered pan; glaze with powdered sugar, and bake in moderate oven. Garnish or fill with vanilla, coffee or chocolate ice cream, assorted and serve on napkin.

MOUSSE AUX FRAISES ROMANOFF

JULES DAUVILLER
CHEF DE CUISINE
PALACE HOTEL
San Francisco, Cal.

Mr. Dauviller was formerly the $10,000 a year dictator of the cuisine in the home of Mr. and Mrs. Harry Payne Whitney in New York. The Whitneys got him from the Grand Hotel in Paris. He served his apprentice-ship in the Cafe de la Paix at Marguery and the Hotel Chabot at the French Capital, before taking responsible posi-tions with the Hotel Riveria at Nice, Italy and the Grand Hotel at Paris. He succeeded to the position of Chef at the Palace in San Francisco upon the resignation of Mr. Ernest Arbogast.

Two baskets of nice strawberries, select the best ones and put aside in bowl with powdered sugar. Take one glass of kummel, one glass of kirsch, and little grated orange peel and let stand on ice for one hour. Pass rest of berries through strainer and add to this half a pound of fine sugar and few drops of lemon juice, one pint of whipped cream, very firm; add then the strained puree of strawberries. Place the whole berries prepared, in a champagne glass with some of the juice, and fill rest of glass with the crushed berries preparation, and let stand in ice box for one hour. Serve with few candied violets on top.

PUNCH GRANITE A L' ANANAS

Take a ripe pineapple, peel, crush well and strain. Make a syrup of one pound of sugar, one pint of water, mix pineapple with it and freeze. Before serving, pour glass of kirschwasser cordial over and serve in sherbet glasses.

J. Dauviller

MARTIN GINDER
CHEF DE CUISINE
HOTEL GREEN
Pasadena, Cal.

Mr. Ginder was apprenticed in France in the best hotels. He was at the New York Athletic Club, the Princeton Club, the old Hotel Metropole, Cafe Savarin and the Vendome Hotel, New York City. He has also held several important positions in the middle west prior to taking his present position.

TUTTI FRUITTI PUNCH

Two cups of milk, five yolks of eggs, two and one-half cupfuls of cream, three-quarters of a cupful of sugar, one-third of a teaspoonful of salt, one tablespoonful of vanilla, one and three-quarters cupfuls of fruit cut in small pieces. Make a custard of the first four ingredients, strain and cool. Add the cream and flavoring, then freeze to the consistency of mush; then add the fruit and continue to freeze. If hard enough, mold and pack in salt and ice for two hours. Candy cherries, figs, raisins and citron may be used.

ORANGE SHERBET

One pint of orange juice, two tablespoonfuls of gelatine, two cupfuls of sugar, one quart of water. Cover the gelatine with a little cold water and soak it half an hour. Boil the sugar and water for five minutes, add gelatine and allow to cool. Add orange juice and freeze.

PISTACHIO ICE CREAM

Pound a half pound of freshly peeped pistachio nuts with two gills of cream. Beat separately twelve raw eggs with ten ounces of sugar, and moisten with a pint of boiling milk. Cook on a slow fire, stirring all the time with a spatula. As soon as the composition is cooked, add the pistachio. Take from fire quickly, and when cold, put in a pint of cream, a little spinach green, just enough to give a nice green color, a little orange flour water, strain through a fine sieve and then freeze.

Martin Ginder

49

JOSEPH
P. CAMPAZZI
CHEF DE CUISINE
ROYAL POINCIANA
Palm Beach, Fla.

Mr. Campazzi was at the Brazilian Court, three years; at the Ponce de Leon, St. Augustine, Fla.; The Breakers, Palm Beach, Fla.; United States Receiving Ship Colorado; Chef to Governor S. J. Tilden, and other important posts as chef.

COMPOTE OF PEACHES A LA VAN DYKE

Boil two quarts of milk. Wash two cups of the best rice, and add to the milk. Add one cup of sugar, and the skin of one orange, cover and cook slowly for thirty minutes. When rice is cooked remove the orange skin, and add one teaspoonful of vanilla flavoring.

Take one can of the best California peaches, and drain part of the syrup into a small saucepan. Put the peaches aside and keep hot. Add to the syrup one small glass of sherry and two tablespoonfuls of sugar. Thicken with peach marmalade or a little cornstarch diluted with sherry. Reduce this syrup until it is very thick. Then add two tablespoonfuls of green chartreuse. Keep warm.

Chop quite fine, a very small quantity of candied fruit, viz., angelica, citron, cherry, almond, etc. While chopping add a little granulated sugar to keep fruit from sticking together. Keep in a saucer ready to use. Prepare a thick cream for decoration. Put the following ingredients in a small saucepan.

Two cups of milk, one dessertspoonful of cornstarch, one dessertspoonful of flour, one teaspoonful of butter, two tablespoonfuls of sugar, one egg yolk, one teaspoonful of vanilla, one drop of green coloring (color should be light green).

Beat this mixture with a small egg whip. Then place on a slow fire, and beat constantly until it comes to a boi . Keep warm until ready to use. Put the rice in a hot round or oval dish. Place the halves of the peaches on the rice. In the center of each half peach put a little currant jelly, and place a blanched almond on the jelly to imitate the pit. Press the cream through a pastry bag with a star-shaped douille, and decorate the rice according to taste. Scatter the candied fruit over the rice and the cream decoration. Pour a little sauce around dish and serve the rest separately. Serve hot. *Joseph P. Campazzi*

BAVAROIS AUX FRAISES

(Bavarian Cream with Strawberries)

Break four yolks of eggs in casserole, two whole eggs well beaten, add boiled milk, one sugar, vanilla flavored. Put on stove until thickens slightly, add few leaves of gelatine. Add crushed strawberries and put on ice in moulds before serving.

GERARD EMBREGTS
CHEF DE CUISINE
CHATEAU FRONTENAC
Quebec, Canada

Prior to coming to America, Mr. Embregts was at the Maison-LeClerc, in Belgium; and the Hotel St. Antoine; the Tavern Renjeaux, in Belgium, the Grand Hotel de L'Empereur at Ostend, Holland, the Berkeley Hotel, Hyde Park Court Club, also at the Embassy de Russe, London.

PECHES CARUSO

(Peaches Caruso)

Take four large peaches, cook in syrup and when cooked, let get cold. Take out pits and fill with pistache ice cream. Close peaches up again, cover with cream chantilly in giving them a cone shape, sprinkle finely chopped pistache over top. Put in the ice box for one hour and serve them on canapies of sponge cake.

HENRI BERGER
CHEF DE CUISINE
FRANKFURTER-HOF
Frankfurt,
A. M. Germany

Mr. Berger has been with the following hotels: Hotel Chatham, Paris; the Hermitage at Monte Carlo, France; the Grand Hotel des Thermes, Salsomaggiore, Italy; the famous Hotel Ritz, Paris, prior to coming to the Frankfurter-hof.

**HENRI
D. FOUILLOUX**
CHEF-STEWARD
**ST. CHARLES
HOTEL**
New Orleans, La.

Mr. Fouilloux served his apprenticeship at the Maison Arwaud of Paris, France. Was later at the Hotel du Rhin, Paris, with Baron de Neaflize at Paris, with Mr. Vayne Mc-Veah — American Ambassador in Rome, with Count Moroni Pecci at Rome, Leo XIII at the Vatican in Rome, Madame Melba in London, for Viscount Bulkeley at Beaumaris in North Wales and at the Grand Hotel in Rome. Coming to this country, he was at the Hollenden Hotel, Cleveland.

COUPE ST. CHARLES

Take four coupe glasses, fill halfways with vanilla ice cream, make a hole in center, place few wild strawberries and good port wine. Cover up and fill coupe glasses with pistache ice cream, garnish with whipped cream, sucred and vanilla flavored and place a nice strawberry on top.

ORANGE PUNCH

Mix the sugar, water, rum and brandy. Add the juice of six oranges, the grated peel of three, and let all infuse for one hour. Then set to cool. When ready to freeze, add one small glass of Cherry Bounce. Serve in hollowed out orange.

LEOPOLD SAUX
STEWARD
**HOTEL
GRUNEWALD**
New Orleans, La.

Mr. Saux is a Grunewald product. He has worked in every department in the back of this hotel, and is considered a very good authority in this line of work.

THEIR ICES, CREAMS AND SWEETS

OTTO GEUTSCH
CHEF DE CUISINE
HOTEL WINDSOR
Montreal, Que. Canada

Mr. Geutsch has been at some of the finest hotels in France, the Hyde Park, London; Cafe Royal, London and also Delmonico's London. The famous chef Monsieur Coffier of the Ritz-Carlton sent him to the Cafe Martin of New York City; later he was at Cafe de la Opera, New York City. While in New York he was awarded five first prizes at the Annual Culinary Exposition and in 1912 received a Medal of Honor by the French Government.

SOUFFLE PALMYRE

Make a vanilla souffle with lady fingers dipped in Curacao and bake in oven for ten minutes. Souffle is made of a half pint of milk, a quarter pound of sugar, two ounces fresh butter, three yolks and four whites of eggs, one ounce farina: Cook milk and sugar, add the farina mixed with a spoonful of cold milk for two minutes and complete mixture off the stove with butter and eggs very firmly beaten.

PECHES POLE DU NORD
(Peaches North Pole)

Poach four nice peaches in vanilla syrup and peel them. Let cool off in the syrup over ice. Dish up in timbal form on layer of vanilla ice cream and pour the following sauce over: one-quarter pint of whipped cream mixed with glass of curacao and a little double cream and serve with some little petit fours.

O. Gentsch,

COUPE CIGARETIERRE

Place some strawberry ice-cream in the bottom of your glass: fix in a crown with some cigaretierre biscuit (Pernod Brand), cut oranges, cherries and grapes into dice, moisten with rum and curacao. Add then additional strawberry ice cream and decorate with pistachio ice cream.

CHOCOLAT CHANTILLY

Iced Chocolat, sprinkled with chopped dry hazelnuts and sweet whipped cream.

JEAN JUILLARD
CHEF DE CUISINE
HOTEL ADOLPHUS
Dallas, Tex.

Mr. Juillard was formerly at Cafe Anglais, Paris; Hotel Hermitage, Monte Carlo; Hotel d'Angleterre, Venice; Savoy Hotel and Princess Restaurant, London; the Plaza, Belmont and Astor Hotels, New York City; Hotel La Salle, Rector's Cafe and University Club, Chicago.

PUNCH DELICES

Raspberry Water Ice with brandied wild cherries in it and perfumed with maraschino.

COUPE FAVORITE

Four candied marrons, eight maraschino cherries, four brandy figs and two slices of pineapple. Cut all in squares, perfume them with chartreuse. Place them in four coupe glasses, fill up the glasses with fresh peach ice cream, decorate the top with whipped cream. Tie a blue ribbon at the stern of the coupes and serve, with a plate of small assorted cakes.

LOUIS
LESCARBOURA
CHEF DE CUISINE
FT. PITT HOTEL
Pittsburg, Pa.

Prior to coming to the Fort Pitt Hotel, Mr. Lescarboura was Chef at the Hotel Marlborough, New York City, and other prominent eastern hotels, and was Entremetier at the famous "Delmonico's Cafe," New York City.

54

JULES BOUCHER
CHEF DE CUISINE
HOTEL ARLINGTON
Hot Springs, Ark.

Mr. Boucher served his apprenticeship at famous French Hotels and Cafes under Chefs world famous, such as Father Thiebout, of the Maison et Chabot of Paris, Chef Cassinin, of the Maisson Dorce, and was at the Restaurant Marguery, Palace Madelaine of Paris and the Cafe Royal of London. Coming to America he was at the Hotel Tourraine, Boston, Auditorium Hotel, Chicago, and the Detroit Club, at Detroit.

BANANA SOUFFLE RUSSE

Peel four bananas, pour kummel over them and pass the soaked bananas into sifted flour. Prepare, one cup powdered sugar, one cup flour, one cup milk, four yolks, one glass liqueur kummel, twelve well beaten whites of eggs and a little salt. Mix the flour and milk, add sugar, kummel and salt, and boil until it shows a certain consistency, stirring well. Take off range and add yolks and bananas. Put into a china dish, then add the whites well beaten and mix slowly. Fill banana forms with mixture mentioned and put in stove for a few minutes until golden brown color and souffle. Sprinkle powdered sugar and serve on napkin.

J. Boucher

PUNCH AU PARFAIT AMOUR

Place one quart of water on the fire with two pounds of sugar until melted, add a teaspoonful of orange flower water, strain and freeze. When nearly stiff, add the snow of eight whites of eggs, mix well and add two pony glasses of Parfait-Amour

SURPRISE PYRAMID, NEAPOLITAINE

G. R. MEYER
CHEF
RECTOR'S
Chicago, Ill.
With finest hotels in Europe, also the Auditorium, Congress and College Inn, Chicago.

Genoise cake is sprinkled with raspberry syrup, cut in shape according to dish. Place in the middle of this foundation a pyramid of French vanilla ice cream three inches in diameter and seven inches high. Along side of this are placed two pyramids of strawberry ice cream, two inches in diameter and six inches high. The three pyramids so formed are covered and decorated with vanilla flavored meringue paste. On top of each is placed a half egg shell also masked and decorated; brown in quick oven. Fill the three egg shells with Kirsch and sprinkle some all over the pyramid. Set on fire the last moment before serving.

FRENCH VANILLA ICE CREAM

One and one-half quarts cream are set on the fire with one pound of powdered sugar and vanilla. When boiling point is reached, remove, take one quart of the boiling cream, scald one dozen egg yolks, previously prepared. Return on fire and heat the whole for four or five minutes. Set in cracked ice until cold and take half of this mixture for vanilla cream. To the remaining, add one-half pint strawberry pulp and two ounces sugar.

ALPS GLORY

Pick and prepare three pints of ripe strawberries, crush half, sweeten and add a dash of cinnamon; let stand for half an hour. Cut six slices of milk bread two-thirds of an inch thick, using only the crumb part of the bread, cut with a round pastry cutter about two and

one-half inches in diameter, and cut these rounds in two through their diameter so as to make twelve half rounds. Butter generously on both sides and dry to a golden color over a slow fire; place on the serving plates, sprinkle with a little powdered sugar and cover with the crushed berries. Place a thin layer of whipped cream over this, desorate with the other half of the berries which were left whole and ornament around with whipped cream. (The whole berries should be rolled in powdered sugar before using.)

G. R. meyer.

JULES KOHLER
CHEF DE CUISINE
HOTEL ADLON
Berlin, Germany
Monsier Jules Kohler
came to the Adlon from
the most elegant and
famous Restaurant in
Paris, the "Cafe de
Paris."

SURPRISE DES CHARTREUX

One-third pint of double cream, same quantity of whipped cream, one and a quarter ounces cake crumbs, one-fifth pint of chartreuse, four leaves of gelatine. Heat double cream, add soaked gelatine and let cool, then add whipped cream and cake crumbs and pour over the chartreuse. Place tart mold on round platter and put in cool place. Take off mold and garnish pudding with strawberries which have been soaked in chartreuse and sucre. Pour sucre adlon over sauce as in Pears Elsa.

J Kohler

CPSIA information can be obtained
at www.ICGtesting.com
Printed in the USA
JSHW081405140623
43226JS00002B/50